Jabbar Wesley
& Partners

Project 180°

BILLIONAIRE
MENTALITY

www.novelcitychamber.com

Published by
Published by Purpose Publishing
1503 Main Street, #168 ♋ Grandview, Missouri
www.purposepublishing.com

ISBN: 978-0-9828379-0-0

Copyright © 2011, Jabbar Wesley
All rights reserved.

Cover designed by Sharon Dailey
Cover Art provided by Single Wing Creative
Editing by Benita Ugoline

Printed in the United States of America

This book, or parts thereof, may not be reproduced, stored in a retrieval system, or transmitted in any form or by means – electronic, mechanical, photocopy, recording, or any other without the prior permission of the publisher.

Inquiries may be addressed to:
www.billionairementality.com

This book is available at quantity discounts for bulk purchases. For more information contact,
www.billionairementality.com

www.novelcitychamber.com

NovelCity Chamber of Innovation Foreword

Billionaire Mentality is a publication of the NovelCity Chamber of Innovation donated by Jabbar Wesley to support fundraising efforts for the
Novel Day Innovation Showcase of 2012

www.novelcitychamber.com

A Note from the Founder

The Novel Day Innovation Showcase is not a mere annual event but it is the entry-point for a novel process of innovation and entrepreneurship. Paradigms are shifting from performance-based thinking to potential-driven investing. Our desire is to champion a cause that will dramatically improve economic environments by providing a revolutionary platform that facilitates information & innovation spillover. The theme for this event is, **"Think novel, take risks!"**

As the economy continues to struggle I personally believe that it is important to encourage entrepreneurs, intrapreneurs, investors, innovators and organizations to embrace and cultivate a culture of risk-taking. Our goal is to provide a platform and network of risk mitigating experts, resources and firms that will increase the risktakers' probability for success. Hence, Novel Day is the beginning of many solutions that will make that a reality. With that said I'd like to thank you for your time and your support in advance!

Kindest regards,

Jabbar Wesley

www.novelcitychamber.com

About Novel City

Novel City is a physical and virtual space for innovation and entrepreneurship. The Novel City Chamber of Innovation was established as a community partner associated with the South Kansas City Innovation Initiative and was designed to empower and stimulate economic innovation and thought leadership. Our mission, vision and value statements are as follows:

The Mission: To maximize the value of unified diversity by developing, embracing and/or promoting multi-cultural innovation through physical and virtual platforms developed and facilitated by our Novel citizens.

The Vision: To increase the rate of innovation in communities, businesses, governments and organizations worldwide in order to provide our next generation of innovators with a legacy of true freedom.

The Value Statement: Novel City as a collective body will uphold a high standard for expertise, integrity, fairness, creativity, openness, trust, humility and excellence. All of which are essential components of a healthy culture that develops globally competitive innovations.

www.novelcitychamber.com

www.novelcitychamber.com

Dedication,

to my Lord and Savior, Jesus Christ;
my beautiful wife, Meka DeMille Wesley;
my sons, (Jay) Phillippe Jabbar Wesley II,
Keyus Allen Wesley and Chase Mekhi Wesley;
Thank you for being patient and
encouraging me to keep dreaming! I Love you!
My parents, Apostle Keith and Pastor Lisa Wesley;
I love you and thanks for the wisdom.
This book is the fruit of everything
you have shared with me.
My brother, Keith A. Wesley, Jr.; I love you!
Thanks for leading me to study wisdom back in 2001.
That was HUGE and the foundation
of my writing of this book.
Special thanks to all of my extended family and true
friends. My corporate family @ Missouri Gas Energy,.
Last but not least, to all of the NovelCity Chamber of
Innovation Board Members, Novel Day 2012 sponsors,
participants, planning team and supporters. We did it!!!
Thank you so much
Thank you for your support!

PS: Rafael Hines! Thanks for telling me to just do it!
It's done!

www.novelcitychamber.com

www.novelcitychamber.com

Contents

Purpose & Objective	12
Instructions	13
Day 1: Leadership	14
Day 2: Wisdom	20
Day 3: Integrity	28
Day 4: Inspiration	34
Day 5: Service	42
Day 6: Balance	48
Day 7: Love	56
Day 8: Potential	62
Day 9: Hope & Humility	70
Day 10: Courage	76
Day 11: Wisdom	84
Day 12: Leadership	90
Day 13: Integrity	98
Day 14: Inspiration	104
Day 15: Initiative	112

www.novelcitychamber.com

Day 16: Courage	124
Day 17: Potential	130
Day 18: Trust	138
Day 19: Respect	144
Day 20: Leadership & Self Knowledge	152
Day 21: Wisdom	158
Day 22: Leadership	166
Day 23: Integrity	172
Day 24: Inspiration	180
Day 25: Initiative	186
Day 26: Love	194
Day 27: Self Recognition	200
Day 28: Balance	208
Day 29: Courage, Faith & Discipline	214
Day 30: Leadership	224
Postscript	232
About the Author	237

www.novelcitychamber.com

Purpose:

Inspiration for writing Billionaire Mentality for Today stems from the following quote of wisdom which has defined my life's path.

"As for the rich in this present age, charge them not to be haughty, nor to set their hopes on the uncertainty of riches, but on God, who richly provides us with everything to enjoy. They are to do good, to be rich in good works, to be generous and ready to share, thus storing up treasure for themselves as a good foundation for the future, so that they may take hold of that which is truly life."

By Paul the Apostle...

Objective:

Billionaire Mentality for Today consists of 180 original quotes. Your objective will be to read 6 quotes per day for 30 days. Interestingly, this book features quotes from my network as well as websites to nonprofit organizations that have innovative and high impact initiatives. As a result of attending to the content of this book you will have invested in a brand new mindset which is the basis for the subtitle: "Project 180".

> The following are 7 instructions for reading
> The Billionaire Mentality for Today.

(These instructions are meant to be recommendations or a guide for the reader).

www.novelcitychamber.com

Instructions:

1. Set aside approximately 10 minutes each morning to read and meditate on the 6 quotes for the day.
2. Think deeply about the content of the quote, but more importantly think about how the book was developed.
3. Think about all the partnerships involved in making this book.
4. Think about all the partners that will be gained as a result of this book.
5. Think about how you will interact with your partners, associates, subordinates, mentors, friends, family and adversaries.
6. Think deeply about how you will apply these principles then set your mind to implement the action plan.
7. At the end of your day, jot down notes that answer the question "How did you do today?" and have fun living with the mind of a righteous billionaire!

www.novelcitychamber.com

DAY 1 Leadership

Thought 1

"Today I will be a marketable product of what hard work produces."

Leadership — DAY 1

Thought 2

"Today I will conduct business and my personal life like I am under surveillance 24 hours a day, 7 days a week."

DAY 1 — Leadership

Thought 3

"Today I will be what I am looking for: loyal, diligent, and honest."

Leadership — DAY 1

Thought 4

"Today I will seek to prove that it pays to PAY ATTENTION."

DAY 1 Leadership

Thought 5

"Today I will make this truth known, "Remaining in silence is the best investment when you have nothing profitable to say."

Leadership — **DAY 1**

Thought 6

"Today I will let it be known that foolish speech is expensive and it will cause you to go bankrupt sooner or later."

How did you do today?

_____
_____
_____
_____
_____
_____
_____
_____

www.novelcitychamber.com

DAY 2 — Wisdom

Thought 1

"Today I will be a pillar of calmness for those who are living an agitated life."

Wisdom — DAY 2

Thought 2

"Today my life will not be the focus of my study. I believe the study of my environment is more important."

DAY 2 Wisdom

Thought 3

"Today is worth more than anything a person on this planet can offer."

Wisdom — DAY 2

Thought 4

"Today I will not allow luck to be a part of my vocabulary. Those who have faith in luck will eventually lose, but labor guarantees some form of success."

www.novelcitychamber.com

DAY 2 Wisdom

Thought 5

"Today I will learn what is needed for today. The matters of tomorrow are worthless at the present time."

Wisdom — DAY 2

Thought 6

"Today I am no longer fearful of death, but I do fear that many will never live because of fear."

How did you do today?

_____
_____
_____
_____
_____
_____
_____
_____

"...The only way to become empowered for tomorrow is to begin taking action **TODAY!**."

Dr. Grace LaJoy, Author
"A Gifted Child in Foster Care"

Website:
www.gracelajoy.com

DAY 3 — Integrity

Thought 1

"Today I will direct all opinions to the truth, only then will I make a judgment."

Integrity — DAY 3

Thought 2

"Today I will work toward perfecting my craft, but I will allow life to perfect my character.."

DAY 3 Integrity

Thought 3

"Today I will live like I deserve to be in leadership. Therefore, I will not give the haters the opportunity to discourage me."

www.novelcitychamber.com

Integrity — DAY 3

Thought 4

"Today I will resist temptations by remembering how priceless my present relationships are."

DAY 3 Integrity

Thought 5

"Today I will live by this truth: "choosing whether to do what is right or wrong is ultimately a life or death situation."

Integrity — DAY 3

Thought 6

"Today I will not build a highway for gossip to be paved on."

How did you do today?

_____
_____
_____
_____
_____
_____
_____
_____

www.novelcitychamber.com

DAY 4 — Inspiration

Thought 1

"Today I will be a slave to discipline. The results will be true freedom."

Inspiration

DAY 4

Thought 2

"Today my faults will be a source of strength to others and to myself."

DAY 4 Inspiration

Thought 3

"Today my optimism says I have the potential to make a billion dollar mistake that would actually be worth billions of dollars."

Inspiration — DAY 4

Thought 4

"Today I will make proactivity my weapon of choice. This weapon will protect me from the unexpected."

DAY 4 Inspiration

Thought 5

"Today I will pursue places where ideas compete and not where people compete."

Inspiration — DAY 4

Thought 6

"Today I will be more than a fundraiser. I am a people raiser."

How did you do today?

_____
_____
_____
_____
_____
_____
_____
_____

"Think of your words as a gift, then determine what kind of gifts you are going to give to others today." May you be empowered by the blessings of God today.

God's Love,
Wayne Albritton
Entrepreneur/Owner
My Private Home Inspector

Website:
www.myprivatehomeinspector.com

DAY 5 Service

Thought 1

"Today I will appreciate and take advantage of the opportunity to be generous."

Service — DAY 5

Thought 2

"Today I will pay attention and respond positively to the less fortunate."

DAY 5 Service

Thought 3

"Today I will not be motivated by prestige but by meeting the needs of others."

Service **DAY 5**

Thought 4

"Today is the day I will pursue matters that benefit others."

www.novelcitychamber.com

DAY 5 — Service

Thought 5

"Today I will use my life for the purposes that are beneficial to all."

Service — DAY 5

Thought 6

"Today I will allow leaders to see truth in my eyes."

How did you do today?

_____
_____
_____
_____
_____
_____
_____
_____

www.novelcitychamber.com

DAY 6 — Balance

Thought 1

"Today I will pursue righteous experiences rather than any kind of opportunity. I believe righteous experiences lead to the best opportunities."

Balance — DAY 6

Thought 2

"Today I will eliminate all business that has no relevant purpose."

DAY 6 Balance

Thought 3

"Today my reactions to positive and negative outcomes will be identical. My reaction will be to assess, accept, and apply what I've learned."

Balance **DAY 6**

Thought 4

"Today I will control my passion with patience and education."

www.novelcitychamber.com

DAY 6 Balance

Thought 5

"Today I will immediately address any sign of anger or anxiety in me by taking a break to focus on what is pleasurable."

Balance — DAY 6

Thought 6

"Today my actions will speak louder than my money."

How did you do today?

_____
_____
_____
_____
_____
_____
_____
_____

www.novelcitychamber.com

"Always the King maker never the King, they can always get a new King."

Tony Grandison
Missouri Department of
Economic Development

www.novelcitychamber.com

DAY 7 Love

Thought 1

"Today I will let love be the blueprint that I will follow. Love never fails."

Love — DAY 7

Thought 2

"Today I will be strong among the strong and a developer of the weak."

---

www.novelcitychamber.com

DAY 7 — Love

Thought 3

"Today my life will give peace and joy
to those I have disappointed."

Love — DAY 7

Thought 4

"Today my desire is to know the value of life."

DAY 7 Love

Thought 5

"Today my mind will be consumed with the value added when my life is connected to others."

Love — DAY 7

Thought 6

"Today I will show my respect and gratitude to those I follow when I am given the opportunity."

How did you do today?

_____
_____
_____
_____
_____
_____
_____
_____

www.novelcitychamber.com

DAY 8 — Potential

Thought 1

"Today I will evaluate my methods of leadership to identify areas of improvement and areas of success."

Potential — DAY 8

Thought 2

"Today I will be content with the pattern my teacher has prepared for me, however, I will not be content with the limitations of that pattern."

DAY 8 — Potential

Thought 3

Today I will look for opportunities to exercise humility."

Potential — DAY 8

Thought 4

"Today I will increase my profit margins of respect as I make large investments in respecting others."

DAY 8 — Potential

Thought 5

"Today I will surround myself with lovers of wisdom. Therefore, I will cut my ties with all that have established themselves in absurdity."

Potential — DAY 8

Thought 6

"Today I will view every person I come in contact with as an opportunity to build a successful relationship."

How did you do today?

_____
_____
_____
_____
_____
_____
_____
_____

www.novelcitychamber.com

"These quotations remind us that in Truth there is life, and Jesus is Truth. This book will provide us with 180 degrees of Freedom."

C.W. Minshew, Consultant
R.W. Beck

DAY 9 Hope & Humility

Thought 1

"Today I will see the possibilities in
what others see as barren."

Hope & Humility — DAY 9

Thought 2

"Today I will admit my mistakes immediately after it is clear that one has been made. This is true humility and a key to effective leadership."

DAY 9 Hope & Humility

Thought 3

"Today I will focus on my purpose for living. I will not try to do what someone else is more suitable for."

Hope & Humility

DAY 9

Thought 4

"Today I will look at my schedule and conclude that nothing on it is more important than what God's wisdom is saying for this season in my life."

DAY 9 — Hope & Humility

Thought 5

"Today I will take note of my limitations and humbly seek assistance."

Hope & Humility — DAY 9

Thought 6

"Today I will find value in exposing my mistakes to the trustworthy. Concealing faults is just as damaging as dying with undisclosed dreams."

How did you do today?

_____
_____
_____
_____
_____
_____
_____
_____

DAY 10 — Courage

Thought 1

"Today I will challenge the fearful to be brave. A culture full of brave hearts has the potential to be a culture of truthfulness, generosity, and compassion."

Courage — DAY 10

Thought 2

"Today I will live. This includes the following, winning, losing, making mistakes, taking risks and facing persecution."

DAY 10 — Courage

Thought 3

"Today I will be grateful for what is contrary to me. Now I know the contrary exists to make me stronger."

Courage — DAY 10

Thought 4

"Today I will exercise my muscle of courage so that when it is most needed a hero will emerge."

DAY 10 Courage

Thought 5

"Today I have decided that giving up on the dream is not an option."

Courage — DAY 10

Thought 6

"Today I would rather have one huge failure than many failures that are small in nature."

How did you do today?

_____
_____
_____
_____
_____
_____
_____
_____

www.novelcitychamber.com

"Life is very stressful at times. Taking time and determining what's useful and what's not can eliminate stress altogether."

Isaiah Townes—Christian Rapper
ChristPusher Records

DAY 11 — Wisdom

Thought 1

"Today I will create memories that will be worth more than every financial transaction I have made combined."

Wisdom — DAY 11

Thought 2

"Today I will go to what I want to know. For it is better to know than to know about."

DAY 11 Wisdom

Thought 3

"Today I will not let security become an obsession. Too much security is free advertisement for your insecurities."

Wisdom — DAY 11

Thought 4

"Today I will listen to good advice from more than just myself. This decision will cause me to help more than just myself in the future."

DAY 11 — Wisdom

Thought 5

"Today I know that my future is based on the company I keep. Therefore, I will join myself to people of integrity."

Wisdom — DAY 11

Thought 6

"Today I will embrace corrective criticisms. Within legitimate complaints solutions can be found, and solutions can be converted to profit."

How did you do today?

_____
_____
_____
_____
_____
_____
_____
_____

DAY 12 Leadership

Thought 1

"Today I will prove that the way up is down. Humble confidence is a key companion of great success."

Leadership — **DAY 12**

Thought 2

"Today I will make it difficult for others to replace me."

DAY 12 Leadership

Thought 3

"Today I will be a trailblazer with the intention to produce more trailblazers."

Leadership — DAY 12

Thought 4

Today I will not allow fear to rob me of a new experience."

DAY 12 | **Leadership**

Thought 5

"Today I will direct others and myself to a higher standard of living."

Leadership — DAY 12

Thought 6

"Today my goal is to execute for those I am living and dying to help."

How did you do today?

_____
_____
_____
_____
_____
_____
_____
_____

"Once we realize we are purely a vessel, the Lord above will use us in so many wonderful ways to uplift others."

Charlie Jones
onewayagent@gmail.com

Website
www.checksonfriday.com

DAY 13 **Integrity**

Thought 1

"Today I will sacrifice my plans if my plans have the potential to assassinate my character."

Integrity — DAY 13

Thought 2

"Today my character is more important than my initiatives."

DAY 13 — Integrity

Thought 3

"Today I will attract people of excellence by being a person of excellence."

Integrity — **DAY 13**

Thought 4

"Today I will be unattractive to flattery and bribes."

DAY 13 — Integrity

Thought 5

"Today I will not sacrifice good character for monetary gain. Money can be good, but it can never be equal to a good name."

Integrity — DAY 13

Thought 6

"Today I will go where I am most needed and there I will find success."

How did you do today?

_____
_____
_____
_____
_____
_____
_____
_____

DAY 14 — Inspiration

Thought 1

"Today I will work with what I have been given. In return, I will produce what has never been seen."

Inspiration — DAY 14

Thought 2

"Today I will showcase my love for what I do. If you don't love what you do, that which you are doing is meaningless."

Inspiration

DAY 14

Thought 3

Today I will set a goal to make every minute I am awake productive."

Inspiration — **DAY 14**

Thought 4

"Today I will respond promptly and properly to every profitable instruction."

DAY 14 **Inspiration**

Thought 5

"Today I will treat my money like a mere associate. Our relationship has no intimacy."

Inspiration — DAY 14

Thought 6

"Today I will let integrity define me."

How did you do today?

_____
_____
_____
_____
_____
_____
_____
_____

www.novelcitychamber.com

www.novelcitychamber.com

"Spiritually speaking, your reality transcends your perception of your current circumstance."

Alex Furlow
Kingdom Life Ministries
www.kingdomlifeministry.webs.com
Email: kingdomlifeministry@hotmail.com

DAY 15 Initiative

Thought 1

"Today I will be the one to start momentum or the one to keep the momentum going and I will strive not to be the one to kill it."

Initiative — DAY 15

Thought 2

"Today I will make an effort to be a dependable source of viable solutions."

DAY 15 — Initiative

Thought 3

"Today I will practice being a servant of all. The benefit of this decision is priceless!"

Initiative — DAY 15

Thought 4

"Today I will seek to prove that a person who views wisdom as a source of amusement is a person who is irrelevant, insignificant and not a factor when major decisions need to be made."

DAY 15 — Initiative

Thought 5

"Today I will keep myself at a safe distance away from fear and ignorance."

Initiative — DAY 15

Thought 6

"Today I will increase the value of integrity."

How did you do today?

_____
_____
_____
_____
_____
_____
_____
_____

www.novelcitychamber.com

"It is so vital to tame the tongue because our words frame our world which is built by relationship."

Lisa Wesley, Co-Pastor
New Life in Christ International Ministries

Website
www.choosenewlife.org

"Self-leadership is the continual alignment of personal motives and methods with the will and character of God."

Todd D. Long, President
Leadership Innovations

Website
www.leadkc.com

"The difference between where you are
and where you want to be is
what you are doing."

Chris Evans, President
T-Shirt Kings, Inc.

Website
www.kingpromo.com

DAY 16 — Courage

Thought 1

"Today I will stand against authority when authority becomes a threat to integrity."

Courage — DAY 16

Thought 2

"Today I will be a fierce competitor of the status quo."

DAY 16 — Courage

Thought 3

"Today I will not live in fear of any potential crisis. Nevertheless, I will continue to prepare for the best and the worst."

Courage — DAY 16

Thought 4

"Today I won't let anything or anyone stand in the way of me getting what is rightfully mine, not even myself."

DAY 16 — Courage

Thought 5

"Today I will stand up for righteousness even if it costs my life. If you are not willing to die for righteousness, your life has little worth."

Courage — DAY 16

Thought 6

"Today I will learn what motivates others so that I can predict and prepare for their actions and reactions."

How did you do today?

_____
_____
_____
_____
_____
_____
_____
_____

DAY 17 — Potential

Thought 1

"Today I will set a goal to master the art of creating successful relationships."

Potential — DAY 17

Thought 2

"Today I will add value to my life with diligence and patience."

DAY 17 Potential

Thought 3

"Today I will vow to live for the possibilities that honesty possesses."

Potential — DAY 17

Thought 4

"Today I will not sleep until I have accomplished something meaningful."

DAY 17 — Potential

Thought 5

"Today I will take note of more than the obvious. People who focus on what the majority observes will be mediocre."

Potential — DAY 17

Thought 6

"Today I will be a threat to injustice."

How did you do today?

_____
_____
_____
_____
_____
_____
_____

"Every time I take a step forward something happens and knocks me back to where I started. Response: when something opposes you or interrupts your normal scheduled program, it doesn't mean that you have to quit because it knocked you back to the starting line. All it means is now you have to redesign your route and go (aka try again)."

Anthony Nelson, Minister
One Purpose

DAY 18 — Trust

Thought 1

"Today I will build on my mentor's legacy of peaceful partnerships."

Trust — DAY 18

Thought 2

"Today I will put a higher value on corrective criticism."

DAY 18 — Trust

Thought 3

"Today I will recognize the value in fairness by investing my resources in those who practice and promote it."

Trust — DAY 18

Thought 4

"Today I will ask God to help me comprehend what is complex."

DAY 18 Trust

Thought 5

"Today I will let go and let God control my decisions."

Trust — DAY 18

Thought 6

"Today I will live like I am convinced that God can do what is impossible for me to do on my own."

How did you do today?

_____
_____
_____
_____
_____
_____
_____
_____

DAY 19 — Respect

Thought 1

"Today I will make an effort to show my associates their worth and value to my life and the lives of others."

Respect | **DAY 19**

Thought 2

"Today I will honor my wise friends by applying their advice to my present situation."

DAY 19 — Respect

Thought 3

"Today I will enjoy the success of others who have succeeded righteously."

Respect — DAY 19

Thought 4

"Today is the day that I will tend to my own business unless I'm asked to get involved in someone else's."

DAY 19 — Respect

Thought 5

"Today I choose to forfeit my right to put substances in my body that have the potential to harm."

Respect — DAY 19

Thought 6

"Today I will focus on elevating my level of productivity instead of wasting time decreasing someone else's."

How did you do today?

_____
_____
_____
_____
_____
_____
_____
_____

"Don't be angry, abrasive or vengeful. These feelings only clutter your mind and waste your precious time."

John B. Kennedy
Tax Consultant

Website
www.jbkennedytaxconsultant.com

DAY 20 Leadership & Self-Knowledge

Thought 1

Today I will be the definition of loyalty."

Leadership & Self-Knowledge — DAY 20

Thought 2

"Today I will seek to develop a culture of trustworthiness."

DAY 20 — Leadership & Self-Knowledge

Thought 3

"Today I will make righteousness and integrity attractive."

Leadership & Self-Knowledge

DAY 20

Thought 4

"Today I will not gravitate toward what is temporary but I will put my trust and interest in what is solid and permanent."

DAY 20 — Leadership & Self-Knowledge

Thought 5

"Today I am grateful for my circumstance. Many are dealing with much worst situations."

Leadership & Self-Knowledge

DAY 20

Thought 6

"Today I will not allow myself to be offended by any individual or group."

How did you do today?

_____
_____
_____
_____
_____
_____
_____
_____

www.novelcitychamber.com

DAY 21 — Wisdom

Thought 1

"Today it's not about me being at the right place at the right time, but it's about me being a righteous person wherever I am."

Wisdom — DAY 21

Thought 2

"Today my focus will be on faithfulness. For seeds of unfaithfulness grow to be trees of jealousy and envy."

DAY 21 — Wisdom

Thought 3

"Today I will trust in nothing but the trustworthy."

Wisdom — DAY 21

Thought 4

"Today I will not be content with where I want to be. I believe being where I should be is sufficient."

DAY 21 — Wisdom

Thought 5

"Today I will cancel the devil's agenda by showing kindness."

Wisdom — DAY 21

Thought 6

"Today I will treat the opportunity to do
what is right as a luxury.
I will enjoy doing it."

How did you do today?

_____
_____
_____
_____
_____
_____
_____
_____

"Really bright people realize that their light is only a reflection of who God is in them."

Michelle Gines, National Administrator
Purpose Publishing, LLC.

Website
www.purposepublishing.com

DAY 22 — Leadership

Thought 1

"Today I will be living proof that possessing enough is greater that desiring more than enough."

Leadership

DAY 22

Thought 2

"Today I will raise the awareness of the unaware."

DAY 22 Leadership

Thought 3

"Today I will be famous for being a strong opponent to ignorance."

Leadership — DAY 22

Thought 4

"Today I will go out of my way to show love to people who consistently cause drama. Then I will sit back and enjoy drama diminish."

DAY 22 — Leadership

Thought 5

"Today I will make an advantage for other human beings. Some choose to take advantage of others only to destroy a valuable friendship that will be much needed in the very near future."

Leadership **DAY 22**

Thought 6

"Today I will speak about the good news in my heart. If I don't have good news, I will find it, then share it."

How did you do today?

_____
_____
_____
_____
_____
_____
_____
_____

www.novelcitychamber.com

DAY 23 — Integrity

Thought 1

"Today I will let nothing leave my mouth that I would hate to come back to my family, friends or myself."

Integrity — DAY 23

Thought 2

"Today I choose to operate in love because hate is like a boomerang. If you throw it, it will come back to you."

DAY 23 — Integrity

Thought 3

"Today I will not be mastered by the opportunities that money presents; therefore, I will master money and become an opportunity."

Integrity — DAY 23

Thought 4

"Today I will form a habit to reject opportunities to deceive."

DAY 23 Integrity

Thought 5

"Today I will take full responsibility for my decisions."

Integrity — DAY 23

Thought 6

"Today I will establish and adhere to the standard of absolute honesty and transparency in my relationships."

How did you do today?

_____
_____
_____
_____
_____
_____
_____
_____

"Team leadership is to draw in and draw out the strengths of others to pursue a purpose together."

Todd D. Long, President
Leadership Innovations

Website
www.leadkc.com

DAY 24 — Inspiration

Thought 1

"Today there is no room for excuses. Excuses are nothing but post dated lies."

Inspiration — DAY 24

Thought 2

"Today I will focus on solutions. Problems are temporary; solutions remain."

DAY 24 Inspiration

Thought 3

"Today I will only fear the results of a lack of wisdom."

Inspiration — DAY 24

Thought 4

"Today I will create a brand for myself and be known as the person who easily forgives."

DAY 24 Inspiration

Thought 5

"Today my actions will be like a billboard that says:
"STILL DOING THE RIGHT THING."

Inspiration — DAY 24

Thought 6

"Today I will use my mind and mouth to liberate and encourage innovation."

How did you do today?

_____
_____
_____
_____
_____
_____
_____
_____

www.novelcitychamber.com

DAY 25 — Initiative

Thought 1

"Today I will use my assets to develop solid and meaningful relationships."

Initiative — **DAY 25**

Thought 2

"Today I will behave like a great investment."

DAY 25 Initiative

Thought 3

"Today I will feed my mind words that produce prosperity."

Initiative — DAY 25

Thought 4

"Today I will consider the consequences of my speech before I speak."

DAY 25 — Initiative

Thought 5

"Today I will help to repair or remove anything or anyone that brings instability in my life."

Initiative — DAY 25

Thought 6

"Today and tomorrow are worthless without the courage to live in them."

How did you do today?

_____
_____
_____
_____
_____
_____
_____
_____

www.novelcitychamber.com

"Innovation is the key to Maximization.
And Integration is the key to Innovation."

Josh Kimbrough
Angel Minds LLC Consulting Group

Founder, Partners X Change
Board Chair, United Races.

<u>Websites</u>
www.InternationalConsultingNews.com
www.PartnersXChange.com

DAY 26 — Love

Thought 1

"Today I will make an effort to give those I will interact with what they genuinely need."

Love | DAY 26

Thought 2

"Today I will reach out to at least one person within my network to show my interest in their well being."

www.novelcitychamber.com

DAY 26 Love

Thought 3

"Today I will take inventory of all that I have, and what I don't need I will give away."

Love — DAY 26

Thought 4

"Today I will be an advocate for the innocent and a companion of the less-fortunate."

DAY 26 Love

Thought 5

"Today I will appreciate my spouse and/or my kids in a unique way."

Love — DAY 26

Thought 6

"Today I will not be the person who constantly takes the credit for team successes. Those who do so should anticipate failure. For those who understand God is the root of your success, get ready for great success!"

How did you do today?

_____
_____
_____
_____
_____
_____
_____
_____

www.novelcitychamber.com

DAY 27 — Self-Recognition

Thought 1

"Today I will address, cultivate and improve the weaknesses that have been identified by me and those who are observing me."

Self-Recognition

DAY 27

Thought 2

"Today my success will be based on my willingness to change what needs to be changed."

DAY 27 — Self-Recognition

Thought 3

"Today I will have no fear of being wrong too early. However, I do have a healthy fear of being accurate too late."

Self-Recognition — DAY 27

Thought 4

"Today I will not allow my assumptions to be my basis for making decisions. Assumptions are nothing more than unwise and uneducated guesses."

DAY 27 — Self-Recognition

Thought 5

"Today I am a failure if by the end of the day; I have zero witnesses of my love for people."

Self-Recognition

DAY 27

Thought 6

"Today I believe tomorrow is worth nothing to me. Now is my net worth."

How did you do today?

_____
_____
_____
_____
_____
_____
_____
_____

"Don't be the weakest link, be the missing link that brings it all together."

Meka DeMille Wesley, CEO
Meka DeMille LLC

Website:
www.mekademille.com
www.demilledesigns.com
www.crunchdontmunch.com

DAY 28 | Balance

Thought 1

"Today I will maximize the value in unified diversity."

Balance

DAY 28

Thought 2

"Today I will be the connection between those with vision and those with provision."

DAY 28 Balance

Thought 3

"Today I will answer the call to lead and to follow."

Balance — DAY 28

Thought 4

"Today I will examine myself to see if I am in humility. If I find that I am not, I will make sure I do what it takes to get back to a humble state."

DAY 28 Balance

Thought 5

"Today I will avoid the repercussions of laziness and reap the benefits of great work ethics."

Balance — DAY 28

Thought 6

"Today I will seek to get an understanding of the perspective of others versus constantly voicing my opinions and demanding attention."

How did you do today?

_____
_____
_____
_____
_____
_____
_____
_____

DAY 29 — Courage, Faith & Discipline

Thought 1

"Today I will not settle for more or less than enough."

Courage, Faith & Discipline — DAY 29

Thought 2

"Today, I will fulfill my obligation to be who I was made to be."

DAY 29 — Courage, Faith & Discipline

Thought 3

"Today I will trust God so that I won't misunderstand His people."

Courage, Faith & Discipline

DAY 29

Thought 4

"Today I will focus on solutions.
Problems are temporary;
solutions remain!"

Courage, Faith & Discipline

DAY 29

Thought 5

"Today I will go to extremes to complete my tasks no matter what obstacles or distractions present themselves."

Courage, Faith & Discipline

DAY 29

Thought 6

"Today I will ask great questions until I receive a great answer."

How did you do today?

_____
_____
_____
_____
_____
_____
_____
_____

www.novelcitychamber.com

> "Just as "who we are" now is the culmination of our life experiences and decisions made, our future is defined by the culmination of work we put in now and willingness to sacrifice to be great."

Eze Redwood
Wings Cafe
Founding Partner

Website:
www.thewingscafe.com

"Today is guaranteed to be graced by surprises that are golden opportunities to explore more talents within, become inspired by creativity and respond with wisdom."

Sharon Dailey, Principal

Sharon-Designs
Visual Communication Consulting

Website:
www.sharon-designs.com

DAY 30 Leadership

Thought 1

"Today I will prove that successful people remain successful because they continue to do what is right, day after day after day."

Leadership — DAY 30

Thought 2

"Today I will seek to be well thought of and a magnet to true success."

DAY 30 | **Leadership**

Thought 3

"Today I will prove that nothing is useless."

Leadership — DAY 30

Thought 4

"Today I will prove that wisdom is the most precious commodity by investing all that I have in it."

DAY 30 | Leadership

Thought 5

"Today I will trust in the belief that hating wisdom is suicide and keeping wisdom to one's self is homicide."

Leadership — DAY 30

Thought 6

"Today I will let it be known that my greatest achievement was when I bowed down and surrendered my life to my Creator."

How did you do today?

_____
_____
_____
_____
_____
_____
_____
_____

www.novelcitychamber.com

"God Bless my Partners!"

Jabbar Wesley-Founder/Executive Director
United Races of America dba
NovelCity Chamber of Innovation

Websites
www.novelcity.org
www.novelstreetjournal.com
www.novelcitychamber.com
www.unitedraces.org

Postscript

In conclusion to Billionaire Mentality for Today, I would like to leave you with a highly impactful poem from my friend, Jason Wattree. Jason is an up and coming author/poet who I believe will change many lives due to his faith in God and his ability to convey timely and significant messages with clarity.

I introduce, Jason Wattree:

Great Gain by Jason Wattree

Jesus Christ the Son of the living God. He was God in Human flesh come down from heaven to save a wretch like you and me from eternal death, although the Pharisees continued to deny his deity. They said, "How can you know Abraham and you're not yet fifty years old?" Jesus replied, "Before Abraham was, I'am. I'am the all existing one, the word of God, the bread of life come down from heaven, and I will lay my life down to save those who will believe in me. This is what needs to be preached to the world today, the gospel of Jesus Christ. But instead the word of life is being handled with hands of greed, not with a sincere heart that when spoken, it brings sinners to their knees. Nah you see we've fell into societies' thoughts, America's mentality to get rich at any cost. We've lost perspective of our true objective, which is to win the lost, not just to get rich so we can serve our lust for material gain always lusting for the next newest thing with no contentment running through our veins because we're not drinking from the well that God sustains, the spirit man. But we hold this world's standard of success in high regard. Could it be that we think we've out-smarted our founding fathers of the faith? To think we no longer have to become martyrs to preach his grace, and I'm not just talking about dying for preaching the faith, I'm also talking about dying to yourself and your lustful ambitions and seek his face so the words you speak can peak and reach every race and nation with much patience us Christians must take in what grace sends our way, but with no hesitation I vow to preach Christ name and added to that I say, "Godliness with contentment is great gain", but that seems to be no longer the aim to obtain of the modern day Christian. Now it's all about three steps to wealth and success, or seven keys to living an abundant life, but very rarely do I hear them preach against sin. They rather teach their congregations on how to get a Benz with no payments, It's a shame ain't it, When the Word of God tells us we shouldn't strive for the material thing that perish. Now I'm not against God's people having nice things but I'm against nice things having God's people to the point that they say you're not in the will of God if you don't have a nice ride or shiny wheels on a big truck, but what about that man that walks three miles to church in Africa has God's will not filled his cup? Surely it has because he braves the hot sun that beams down on his dark mask, and he can't afford for his eyes protected by shaded glass. People of God, this is sad! We need to get back to what pleases our dad, which is the will of God and that is to believe on the Lord Jesus Christ and to love one another. That should be the aim of every Christian that's listening to what I'm spittin Christ the risen has given us the wisdom to train and not to retain or keep inside because no lie can stay alive when us Christians speak the word with no compromise. So let us not strain our brains on how we can cleave to fortune and fame, but let us concentrate on preaching Christ name and added to that I say, "Godliness with contentment is great gain."

Original prose—Copyright © 2011, Jason Wattree

Contact Jason at:
jasonwattree@yahoo.com
www.facebook.com

Jabbar Wesley
& Partners

Project 180°

BILLIONAIRE
MENTALITY

www.novelcitychamber.com

About the Author

Jabbar's corporate background is rooted in the natural gas industry holding a position as the Economic Development and Residential Representative with Missouri Gas Energy. Jabbar has been a major part in developing and maintaining effective working relationships with 155 cities as well as local, county, state and federal economic development organizations, architects and real-estate developers. Jabbar also plays an important role in major business attraction projects for large commercial, industrial and residential projects.

Jabbar is also the Founder of Novel City Chamber of Innovation a dba of United Races of America which is a community economic development organization focused on maximizing the value of unified diversity through community events, education resource development services and business incubation and consulting. Jabbar holds a degree in Economics from the University of Missouri's College of Arts and Sciences in Kansas City and has studied Leading Innovation and Change at Robert Kennedy College of Zurich, Switzerland.

www.novelcitychamber.com

"As for the rich in this present age, charge them not to be haughty, nor to set their hopes on the uncertainty of riches, but on God, who richly provides us with everything to enjoy. They are to do good, to be rich in good works, to be generous and ready to share, thus storing up treasure for themselves as a good foundation for the future, so that they may take hold of that which is truly life."

Apostle Paul of Tarsus

www.ingramcontent.com/pod-product-compliance
Lightning Source LLC
Chambersburg PA
CBHW051425290426
44109CB00016B/1440

www.ingramcontent.com/pod-product-compliance
Lightning Source LLC
Chambersburg PA
CBHW011150290426
44109CB00025B/2551